Creswell

Published by

Librario Publishing Ltd

ISBN: 1-904440-91-6

Copies can be ordered via the Internet
www.librario.com

or from:

Brough House, Milton Brodie, Kinloss
Moray IV36 2UA
Tel /Fax No 00 44 (0)1343 850 617

Creswell

To Ted, the navigator

Librario

FOREWORD

Step aside just this once, all of you, and let a mere Loon tell you about this splendid book! It is a great honour for me to be writing these words. I do at least share an understanding of the creative life and know what fun it is to be lucky enough to be able to make people smile! I love original thinkers too, and in particular original artists; Jean Dinsdale-Young, alias Creswell, has combined these two talents with her wonderful sense of humour to produce cartoons that are so uniquely and distinctively hers! Hoorah! Hooray! Haroodle!!

Laughter is the medicine that we all need, one dose cures all known disease and replenishes a vital part in our bodies that nothing else can reach in the same way! This collection of cartoons is such a draught, and it epitomises so many aspects of life: the freezing Scottish baronial castles or stalking that elusive Highland stag, St.Paul writing his epistle to the Thistleonians...I love it, it's so simple but it really makes me laugh! But take a second look at this work, the draughtsmanship, the compositions, the detail and the ability to draw and paint, because she has captured her subject with great talent, freedom and a real twinkle. She's good at it! When you own a Creswell cartoon, and of course this book, it is inevitable that you will occasionally witness an explosion of laughter coming from the 'small room' – from that captive audience! What a satisfying feeling that is for all concerned!!

So from a fellow doodler, I congratulate Jean on the production of this wonderful collection of cartoons...keep 'em coming! And as you take this medicine, you too will become well within!!

Over to you now. Enjoy!

INTRODUCTION

In my experience cartoons are rather low in the pecking order of Art. Top place must go to pickled sharks and unmade beds. Graffitti at the bottom perhaps, although even that is on the rise. The Old Masters sit somewhere in between. But cartoons, NO! Vulgar, nasty and sometimes – ha – ha – HA! funny.

When I was at school a long time ago, I was made to sleep alone in a huge dark dormitory up in the roof. Everybody else cowered under blankets on the ground floor with German bombers thundering overhead and all because I had made a little book of cartoons of the staff with rhymes underneath. One I remember was of a large lady dancing on a desk in her Directoire knickers. The complaint supposedly was of wasting precious paper in wartime, and that I alone might be accused of single- handedly losing the war, if we did.

An earlier headmistress had sent for my mother to complain that I was always drawing people with sinister faces. And, what's more, from the FEET UP. How better could she have described a child's eye view of the world? Luckily my mother had the sense to laugh instead of having me locked up.

Cartoons run in our family. One of my brothers could catch exaggerated likenesses in a few brilliant lines, but preferred to be a farmer. A great great grandfather, laird of an ancient estate in Ayrshire, drew a series of pictures entitled 'The Cockney Sportsman' in 1800, when a fresh wave of the nouveau riche was heaving into view. They were engraved by Gilray and published by Mrs. Humphreys in London. From my father's side of the family I inherited a real sense of the ridiculous, for better or for worse.

I went to Art schools at Liverpool and Wimbledon - plenty of life-drawing and anatomy. One model had a snake tattooed round his waist which grew and shrank as he breathed. Once he stood on his hands on a high stool to show off his marvellous muscles and all the lights failed and there was a terrible crash in the darkness.

One tutor would sit throughout lessons with his feet on a desk, eyes closed and only the soles of his feet showing - rather different and liberating after that strict boarding school.

I then did a short spell in advertising mostly for the Co-op and our local paper. Cartoons were not the thing there, being really diametrically opposed to each other. Advertising exists to show things as they are not. I was told triumphantly by the sales manager that my (I thought) funny ad for Gift Tokens had failed to shift a single one. Likewise a rather nice little Bewickish illustration of a village funeral for the Co-op Funeral Parlour was quickly vetoed and a tasteful bunch of lilies substituted with the syrupy caption : 'In gracious tribute to your Loved One.' This caused much hilarity at home but ran for years in the Essex County Standard. Another I remember (that won a prize for the studio, not for me) was of a balloon going up with 'Up goes the dividend - now 1/ 6.'

Next came marriage and a move to Vancouver Island from where we returned twelve years later with our four children in a home made boat built of chicken wire and cement, actually a beautiful 60 foot ketch called Hornpipe. That's another story. We sailed into western Inverness-shire and dropped the anchor. I took up painting again. Magnificent scenery but also plenty of jokes.

One day I happened upon a cartoon competition in the *Scottish Field* which I was glancing through in a supermarket in Inverness. I had tried sending them some before and back came a rejection slip with a sharp comment from the Ed. telling me to study my market. I dusted them off, redrew some bits and sent them off again. This time there was an impressive row of judges including the Director of the Scottish National Portrait Gallery. To my sheer astonishment they declared me the winner, the clear winner what's more, out of 86 entrants and at the grand prize giving (to which my husband and I were carried in a white Mercedes) the judges were equally astonished that I should turn out to be a woman. "How did you make them so *Scottish Field*?" I was asked ,which I couldn't answer because I almost never encountered that glossy magazine in our remote corner of the country.

As a result of this lucky chance I was given a little slot in the *Glasgow Herald's* womans' page on Saturdays and interviewed by various papers, one of which asked what it felt like to have your work used for wrapping the fish and chips. This made me think a bit and we decided to sell them, worked up and detailed, printed in colour, mounted and framed., which we have done for the last 12 years. We sell them at country fairs and Christmas fairs and anywhere suitable.

Here at last are some of them huddled together in a BOOK which I hope you will enjoy.

Creswell

"Hostages, idiot! I said HOSTAGES!"

"—and what was I _supposed_ to do?"

"Hunter-gatherers, Mabel — hunter-gatherers."

"It says to keep the roots cool....."

"Fall out that woman not in uniform!"

"... supposed to be haunted? What nonsense say I!"

"But Æsop – these are absolutely FABULOUS!"

"Come ON Hector — only another ten miles!"

"Me wear a kilt? You must be joking"

"I'm beginning to think they're going to see me out...."

"But you KNEW I wanted picture windows!"

" They say he's FRIGHTFULLY good ---"

"No, madam, this is where civilisation BEGINS!"

"They cut down all the trees for 'Ease of Maintenance'!"

"I sometimes think driving on to these new Ro-Ros is like entering the jaws of some great fish ...."

"At least you can count on there being no crocodiles!"

"Never saw a beast all day . . . . . ."

'Sorry about your awful weather — it's in the 80's here and growth's tremendous ---."

"Women priests, women bishops — and now THIS!"

"Reckon we're safe enough here, boy!"

"It would seem to relate to some ethnic minority".

"I'm a firm believer in Method ....!"

"Say– can you tell me where I can see heather–r–r?"

"Naturally I only shoot them flying..."

"Good—ee! A fine day for the garden opening!"

"Walk ON!"

M-A-R-M-A-L-A-D-E-O-R-A-N-G-E-S-N-O-W-I-N.

"Come on Felix. Meet the gorillas in the mist!"

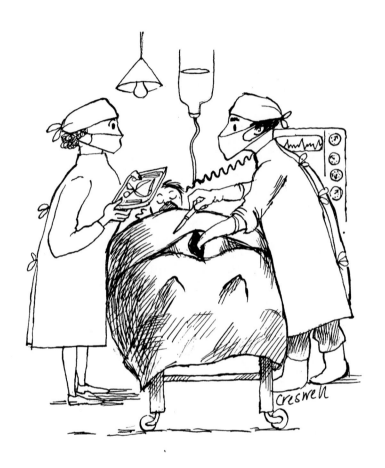

" His heart's in the Highlands —
    His heart is not here ! "

P'SST!

"The white settlers and the blue mafia I suppose."

"Insomnia? Never! I just count my birthdays!"

"So much for global warming....!"

"Do you think we should tell them about our septic tank?"

"And they tell me the meaning of Hogmanay is lost in the mists of antiquity!"

"*I just love the new winter collection!*"

"I understood from watching the Monarch of the Glen that this is what one wears in the Highlands!"

"I name this child WWW Dot.....!"

A hunting morning

My friends are going hunting and leaving me behind,
For vulpicide, this morning, is
Not what I have in mind.
I'm up and down the staircase like a yo-yo on a string,
I'm hunting for my credit cards, I'm hunting for my ring,
I'm hunting for my library books, I'm hunting for my pen,
I'm hunting for that recipe to marinade a hen.

I scrabble in the cupboards and tunnel like a mole,
Where DID I put my spectacles?
O, what a glory hole !
My friends are all enjoying a gallop on the heath
But I am in the darkness in the cupboard underneath the stairs.
My blood is boiling,I'm as stressed as any fox.
Oh WHY so many bottles? And WHAT is in that box?

My saddle's in the stable and my horse is in the field,
His eyes are pointing north and south,his rolling eyes are peeled,
His neighing sounds falsetto and he's working up a sweat
My horse is now connected to the Horses' Internet.

He's heard the hounds,he's heard the horn,
And now he's seen the hunt,
It seems to him a miracle, a most tremendous stunt.
He's thundering across the ground,he's rising in the air,
He's jumped that most enormous gate with several feet to spare.
I glimpse him through the window but instead of feeling pride,
I'd like to wring his noble neck,
Commit equestricide.

Instead of hunting long-lost things I'm tearing through the gorse
And on this hunting morning
I'M A-HUNTING FOR MY HORSE !

"Do let me show you our wild garden —!"

"Looks like they're inaugurating the new function suite!"

The Afternoon Bath

Hallo ? You're going shooting ? Yes – I'll be shooting too!
You didn't know I had a gun? I haven't – not like you.
You're shooting at a castle ? Among the great and good?
With belted earls and girls with pearls and princes of the blood
And pheasants to be driven from that hundred acre wood?

With scarlet shooting stockings and tweeds of Eau de Nil,
Your black and yellow Labradors respectfully to heel,
The pheasants will be dazzled and waver in their flight.
Your gun will swing so gracefully and
BANG ! BANG ! – left and right ,
They'll crash to earth like shuttlecocks ,
The dust their beaks to bite.

I'd LOVE to come on Sunday to feast upon your prey,
But sadly I'll be busy on that celebration day.
I said I would be shooting - and on the Sabbath too !
I'll be shooting down the rapids in my Indian canoe !

The Organic Gardener.

"A Tidy desk is an empty mind!"

"I really wanted something to wear for committee meetings."

"And this, of course, is a fake....."

"Looking for his forebears, I expect."

"You know — Delia Smith could change our lives!"

"Yes — well — we prefer to call it ground cover ...."

"It's Bonnie Prince somebody-or-other Miss Flora — wanting a lift."

Creswell

Creswell "the second cup."

"Remember that tiny shoot of groundcover you gave me ---?"

"Change the course of history — me?"

"But I am — _am_ — financially!"

"...and this is my brother dressed as Father Christmas!"

"My grandmother, in fact."

"Really George — those cherubs!"

"Seems he's writing an epistle to the Thistleonians".

"All this tommy-rot about Father Christmas..."

"I always thought they WERE women!"

"Long yellow fruit — something A, something A, something A ....?"

"She seems to have found herself at last!"

The endless Pibroch

"Prince Charles won't like yours, Fred".

"Hallo — is that the Orphanage?"

"But it is MARVELLOUSLY cool in summer!"

"It's the arms I hate doing."

"The trouble is — he can't remember whether he's a Jacobite or a Hanoverian ...."

"You know Annie, I think we're beginning to slow down."

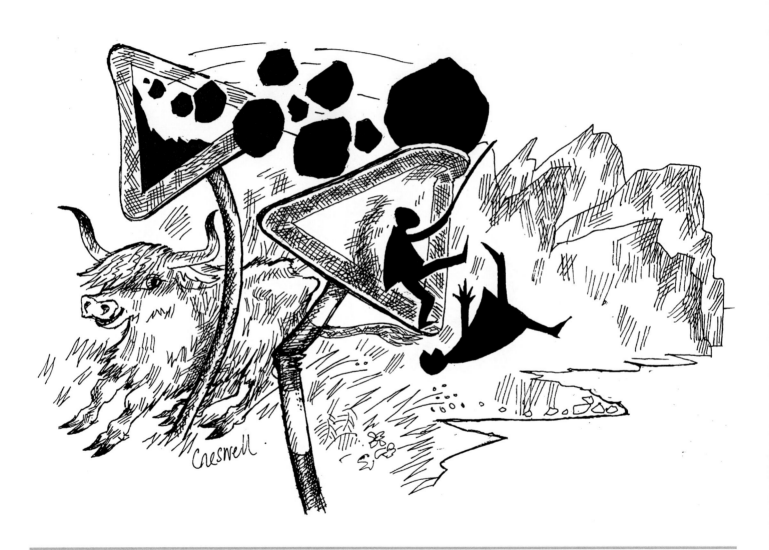

"O.K. Fred — now the oilrig."

"To be perfectly honest I can't crack it."

"It's not fair really — he uses colonic irrigation."

"Ban blood-sports Foxey? What shall we do then?"

"NEIGHbours of course!"

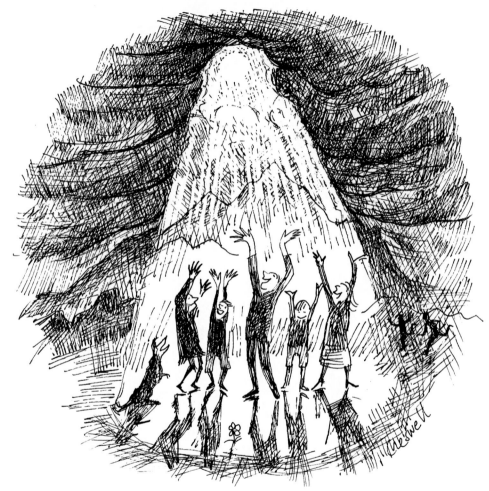

Summer comes to the Highlands

"Well, you have to, don't you!"

"Edwin does blood sports and I do dried flowers..."

"My word! You HAVE matured!"

"He's like the Ancient Mariner — but he doesn't stop at one in three — he stops at them all!"

"A postcard from Cousin Maud to thank us
for having her to stay for six months—"

"It's Christopher Columbus — bringing us the benefits of Western Civilisation!"

Well I'm unanimous — and that's all that matters!

"That dog watches too much television!"

"Well — they did SAY 'frog patches'..."

"Congratulations, Mrs. West — you have just been awarded the Turner prize!"

The sporting Artist .

"... and this is your Aunt Buttercup — completely pickled!"

"My dear — I feel utterly VITRIFIED!"

"Good sponsorship **is** of course, absolutely vital—!"

"...and FINALLY there will be harping lessons in the vestry for those of riper years."

"You're _SO_ pigheaded!"

"She obviously knows the way to a man's heart!"

"I **KNOW** they said 'come as you are'!"

"Hauntin' first —
then 'hootin' & swishin' you bet!

"Fourteen bedrooms and no bathroom!"

"I could never <u>VOTE</u> labour!"

"Ah! You must be the pollen Count!"

"A bit too <u>tidy</u> — if you ask me!"

"I wish he'd be more specific —
 I don't know whether to laugh or beat the war drum!"

Life in the Highlands — wind-powered television!

" Speed bonny boat —!"

"A memory transplant? How splendid!"

"This must surely add enormously to our knowledge of the Picts—!"